In this season of waiting

Daily readings for Advent

GW00775674

In this season of waiting

Daily readings for Advent

Thom M Shuman

wild goose
publications www.**ionabooks**.com

First published 2023 by
Wild Goose Publications
Suite 9, Fairfield
1048 Govan Road, Glasgow G51 4XS, Scotland
A division of Iona Community Trading CIC
Limited Company Reg. No. SC156678
www.ionabooks.com

ISBN 978-1-80432-313-7

Cover photo © Neirfy | Dreamstime.com

The publishers gratefully acknowledge the support of the Drummond Trust,
3 Pitt Terrace, Stirling FK8 2EY in producing this book.

Overseas distribution
Australia: Willow Connection Pty Ltd, 1/13 Kell Mather Drive, Lennox Head NSW 2478
New Zealand: Pleroma, Higginson Street, Otane 4170, Central Hawkes Bay

Printed by Bell & Bain, Thornliebank, Glasgow

Contents

Introduction   7

First week of Advent   9

First Sunday of Advent: God who does cartwheels   10
First Monday of Advent: God who lights the way   12
First Tuesday of Advent: God who never forgets us   14
First Wednesday of Advent: God who watches on hillsides   16
First Thursday of Advent: God who is still with us   18
First Friday of Advent: God of the forgotten   20
First Saturday of Advent: God of grace and sharing   22

Second week of Advent   25

Second Sunday of Advent: God who never blows out the light   26
Second Monday of Advent: God who tries to slow us down   28
Second Tuesday of Advent: God whose heart is filled
with stained glass in its cracks   30
Second Wednesday of Advent: God who watches in the night   32
Second Thursday of Advent: God of abundant creation   34
Second Friday of Advent: Composer of all wonders   36
Second Saturday of Advent: God who is our balm   39

Third week of Advent   41

Third Sunday of Advent: Delight of the universes   42
Third Monday of Advent: Heart of our hearts   44
Third Tuesday of Advent: Imagination beyond compare   46
Third Wednesday of Advent: Sharer of your heart's abundance   48

Third Thursday of Advent: Omnipotent God   50
Third Friday of Advent: God of those we ignore too often   52
Third Saturday of Advent: God who quilts a people   54

Fourth week of Advent   57

Fourth Sunday of Advent: God of overflowing intimacy   58
Fourth Monday of Advent: God who is coming   60
Fourth Tuesday of Advent: God of disruption   62
Fourth Wednesday of Advent: God who is speaking to us   65
Fourth Thursday of Advent: God our love, our voice, our hope   66
Fourth Friday of Advent: God of compassion   68
Fourth Saturday of Advent: God of Light   70

Christmas Eve: Whispering God   74

Christmas Day: God in community, Holy and One   78

Meditation   80

Introduction

In 2020, the church I am blessed to serve, like just about everyone else, 'lost' the season of Advent. We could no longer gather together in person. We couldn't light the candles of the Advent wreath in church. We couldn't sing the Advent hymns and carols, except in our homes.

2021 was a little bit better, as we could now gather in person, if folk were fully vaccinated and boostered, but singing the beloved music was a challenge, since we still needed to wear masks. The challenges of trying to observe this holy season in the time of pandemic still wears at our hearts and souls.

As I tried to be faithful during those seasons, I wrote daily reflections on scripture readings (some taken from a lectionary, others Bible passages which I felt appropriate for particular days), and put together a series of prayers for the lighting of the Advent candles in the home each evening. *In This Season of Waiting* came out of that discipline and time.

You can literally light candles while following the days here, or light them in your heart and mind. Whichever way, they will never be extinguished, even when we pack up our wreath, our candles and our Advent prayers for another year.

Thom M Shuman

First week of Advent

First Sunday of Advent: God who does cartwheels

For you yourselves know very well that the day of the Lord will come like a thief in the night.

1 Thessalonians 5:2

Come,
Shoplifter of our foolishness,
to steal away our arrogant pride
so that we learn to trust
completely in God

come,
Mugger of our moments,
to take away our selfishness
so that we may notice
the strugglers around us

come,
Cat Burglar of our souls,
to tiptoe away with our fears
so that we may surround
others with hope and grace

come,
Pickpocket of our hearts,
to relieve us of our prejudices
so that we may see
strangers as beloved siblings

come,
Thief in the night,
to steal us away from
death's uncrackable safe
so that we may become gifts
to those whose lives are empty

+

We light the candle of expectation
in this season of waiting,
God who does cartwheels
in our self-righteous souls,
knowing you will take our longings
for that perfect
greeting card/holiday movie Christmas
and turn them into
a maternity ward
where the poor are given
the best care

a home where the forgotten
are welcomed after everyone
has turned them away

and a Saviour who refuses
to do what we think
should be done.
Amen

First Monday of Advent: God who lights the way

When they had come near Jerusalem and had reached Bethphage, at the Mount of Olives, Jesus sent two disciples, saying to them, 'Go into the village ahead of you, and immediately you will find a donkey tied, and a colt with her; untie them and bring them to me. If anyone says anything to you, just say this, "The Lord needs them." And he will send them immediately' ...

The disciples went and did as Jesus had directed them ...

Matthew 21:1–3, 6

If only
we would go and
do as you direct us,

those in poverty
   would become philanthropists

little children
   would become our teachers

the voiceless
   would be the guest speakers

the broken
   would become healers of us all

hatred would
   not gain a foothold in our hearts

misery would
   not find a home anywhere

evil would
   become an extinct species

compassion would
   be second nature

love would
   be our constant companion

if only ...

+

We light the candle of journeying
in this season of waiting,
God who lights the way,
trusting you will guide us
(however reluctant we are)
to those who are weary of war,
to all who hunger to feast on gentleness,
to the one we have walked past,
to your children who are kicked out
of the communities we have shaped.
Amen

First Tuesday of Advent: God who never forgets us

Therefore I intend to keep on reminding you of these things, though you know them already and are established in the truth that has come to you. I think it right, as long as I am in this body, to refresh your memory …

2 Peter 1:12–13

Come
God of our memories,
to remind us of who we are
and what we are called
to be in this life

come
God who whispers in our souls,
to sing over and over
that we are still your
Beloved

come
God of our mountaintops,
that your grace warms
us in the winter of our lives

come
God who sends mentors,
so we can find
our way back to your heart

come
God of the stumblers,
to pick us up when
we trip over our untied
laces of faith

come
God of the journey,
so we may help others
to remember what
this season of holiness
truly means.

Come …

+

We light the candle of remembrance
in this season of waiting,
God who never forgets us,
for though we may know
the story so well we can
recite it without any prompting,
still, it can sweep us off our feet,
still, it can take our breath away,
still, it can move us to tears,
still.
Amen

First Wednesday of Advent: God who watches on hillsides

Thus says the Lord: As the shepherd rescues from the mouth of the lion two legs, or a piece of an ear, so shall the people of Israel who live in Samaria be rescued, with the corner of a couch and part of a bed.

Amos 3:12

When
we have fallen into
the pit, the walls
as slick as glass
and everyone
walking by
tossing platitudes
down to us,
you jump in
and grab our hands,
saying,
'trust me,
I know the way out'

when
we are caught in
sin's enticement, you
firmly grasp its
jaws,
prying them apart
until we can
pull loose

when
we are waylaid
by death, wrapped
in its cold embrace,
you shine a
Light
so we can see
the footsteps
in the dust
which lead us
to
you.

+

We light the candle of the shepherds
in this season of waiting,
God who watches on hillsides,

not just the ones who wear
the fancy garb in church
but those with runny noses
and flapping bathrobes in pageants

not just those who serve on boards
making the decisions
but the folk unclogging the loo
and putting the bins out by the curb.
Amen

First Thursday of Advent: God who is still with us

He brought me out into a broad place;
* he delivered me, because he delighted in me.*

Psalm 18:19

You could level
the mountains you shawled
in snow
to get our attention,
but you
bend down to take
sin's pebble
out of our shoes

you could send
winter's wind
to rattle our
windows,
but you
caress us with
a cool breeze on
the hottest of days

you could push a
wave to knock us off
our pious pedestals,
but you
hold a cup of water
to our parched
lips

you could do
anything,
and everything,
to deliver us,
but instead,
you became
us.

+

We light the candle of Immanuel
in this season of waiting,
God who is still with us,
in the children chalking messages
of hope on neighbourhood sidewalks

in the young couple dropping off
groceries to old folk isolated in apartments

in communities living out
an incarnational faith
in a time of unparalleled separation.
Amen

First Friday of Advent: God of the forgotten

Seek good and not evil,
that you may live;
and so the Lord, the God of hosts, will be with you,
just as you have said.
Hate evil and love good,
and establish justice in the gate ...

Amos 5:14–15a

When it is easier
to condemn the cruel
than to acknowledge
how our privilege shields
us from noticing the needy,
come

when we talk
a good game
about justice
but then sit on
the sidelines,
come

when we have
trouble getting up
off our apathies
and going to serve,
come

just as you said,
Lord of our lives,
come to be with us

come ...

+

We light the candle of justice
in this season of waiting,
God of the forgotten,
as CEOs hold on to bonuses
and workers lose their safety net

as the needy sit in long lines hoping
to get enough food for a week
while the privileged know
they will never lack anything.
Amen

First Saturday of Advent: God of grace and sharing

Then he said to them, 'Whose head is this, and whose title?' They answered, 'The emperor's.' Then he said to them, 'Give therefore to the emperor the things that are the emperor's, and to God the things that are God's.'

Matthew 22:20–21

As the haves
move up the
wealthiest list
and the nots
slide deeper into
nothing,
i read of your
heart
breaking
for the poor

as the powerful
stockpile more and more
and the vulnerable
have less and less,
you speak to me of
giving away everything
i have

as the spin doctors
medicate us with
platitudes and bias

and the voiceless
can find no advocates,
i hear your words
of the last becoming
first

when i look at you,
wondering
which side to take,
which way to go,
you take a coin
(with 'grace' stamped
on one side
and 'greed' on the other)
out of your
pocket
and flipping it
into the air,
whisper,

'you call it'

+

We light the candle of anticipation
in this season waiting,
God of grace and sharing,
knowing there will come that day
when worries are turned
into bouquets of wonder

when fears are transformed
into a fountain of kindness

when our time becomes
a history of grace and sharing.
Amen

Second Week of Advent

Second Sunday of Advent: God who never blows out the light

Make me to know your ways, O Lord;
*   teach me your paths.*
Lead me in your truth, and teach me,
*   for you are the God of my salvation;*
*   for you I wait all day long.*

Psalm 25:4–5

When we come and
sit down with you
on the beach where
you are grilling some fish,
to ask you the age-old
question, you
take our buckets full
of sand and, slowly
pouring them out so that
every grain glows
in the sunset, whisper,
'that's how many times
you need to forgive'

as we climb up
into your lap and begin
to tell you about all
the folk, especially family,
who disappointed us today,

you reach down and
pick up a picture book,
and opening it, ask,
'have I told you the story
of the dad and his two kids?'

+

We light the candle of hospitality
in this season of waiting
for hearts which swing open
to include those we ignore

for hands which give
hugs to the folk
we have missed

for feet which walk beside all
who've been left alone

for souls which offer
safe spaces and places
as you do for us,
God who never blows out the light,
but runs to welcome us home.
Amen

Second Monday of Advent: God who tries to slow us down

On the glorious splendour of your majesty,
and on your wondrous works, I will meditate.

Psalm 145:5

Being bounced on
the white-water rapids,
gazing at nebulae
in distant galaxies,
tasting the first snowflakes
on my tongue,
all creation can stun me
with its complexity
as well as simplicity

but watching the
ginger cat sitting
still for endless moments,
teaches me your patience

noticing a little boy
sharing half his lunch
with a rough sleeper
in the park,
i see your face

paying attention to
the silent carols a mother
sings to her child

in the hospital,
i hear your voice

and as i lie on my
bed counting my blessings
and recalling my moments,
i drink from the deep wells
of your Spirit.

+

We light the candle of stillness
in this season of waiting,
God who tries to slow us down,

for in such a hurry to get
all our cards and packages
sent out before the deadline

for in our rush to buy just
the perfect presents for all

for in the hustle-bustle of our days

we may just miss the silence
which carries the soft whispers
of the grace which can fill
emptiness.
Amen

Second Tuesday of Advent: God whose heart is filled with stained glass in its cracks

Our soul waits for the Lord;
*   he is our help and shield.*
Our heart is glad in him,
*   because we trust in his holy name.*
Let your steadfast love, O Lord, be upon us,
*   even as we hope in you.*

Psalm 33:20–21

It would make it easier,
God for whom we wait,
if the psalmists had been clearer:
'I waited for the Lord for a year.
I waited until the harvest was over.
I waited until ...'

but maybe
they discovered, as we do,
that the waiting
is a just-ploughed field
where you plant seeds of life

that the waiting
is the thin place
where we glimpse your hope,
taste your grace,
are warmed by your love,
are made new by your justice

maybe
it is in the waiting
that we finally find you,
God who is worth the wait.

+

We light the candle of sadness
in this season of waiting,
God whose heart is filled
with stained glass in its cracks

for all the folk who sit staring
at the empty chair across the table

for all whose jobs are not coming back

for all for whom this season
is not bright and sparkly, but
is the bluest Christmas
they have ever known.
Amen

Second Wednesday of Advent: God who watches in the night

When I saw him, I fell at his feet as though dead. But he placed his right hand on me, saying, 'Do not be afraid; I am the first and the last, and the living one. I was dead, and see, I am alive forever and ever; and I have the keys of Death and of Hades.'

Revelation 1:17–18

You whisper the
promise
as we take our
first breath,
our lungs expanding
with Spirit's gift

you put your arms
around us,
murmuring it
as you gently
bandage our
souls from
sin's bullying

you write the
words
on a piece of
paper,
putting it in our
lunchbox
on that first day
of school

you shout it
at the top of your
lungs,
when we are
deafened
by the decibel-breaking
din of late bells
and angry teachers

you sigh the
promise
as we take our
last breath,
the Spirit cradling us
to carry us home to
you:

'do not be afraid'

+

We light the candle of comfort
in this season of waiting,
God who watches in the night,
trusting that the only things
under our beds are dust bunnies,
the only scary monsters
in the closet are smelly shoes,
that the baby whose birth we celebrate
will cradle us in
resurrection love.
Amen

Second Thursday of Advent: God of abundant creation

'For you tithe mint, dill, and cummin, and have neglected the weightier matters of the law: justice and mercy and faith. It is these you ought to have practised without neglecting the others ...'

Matthew 23:23

When the privileged
have so much justice
available to them,
  why do we think
  it too much to offer
  even a tenth of it
  to those who have nothing?

when i am so quick
to reach out and
demand you care for
me every time i bump
my pride in the shadows,
  how can i think it too
  much to give even
  a bandage to the broken?

when i am asked
to tithe my faith,
is it too hard
  because i am
  convinced

that the little seed
in my soul
is not enough,
even for me?

+

We light the candle of generosity
in this season of waiting,
struggling to admit that we
who think we are poor
have so much more than
so many around us

that we who have so much
could do a better job of sharing,
God of abundant creation.
Amen

Second Friday of Advent: Composer of all wonders

Praise the Lord!
Praise the Lord from the heavens;
    praise him in the heights!
Praise him, all his angels;
    praise him, all his host!

Psalm 148:1–2

Little kids
who sing carols
with their hands,
and grandparents
living in their childhood
Christmases –
praise God

geese announcing
their departure times
for the south,
and chickadees ice skating
in birdbaths –
praise the Lord

giraffes craning
their necks towards
the winter moon,
and bears hibernating
in winter's cradle –
praise God

hawks soaring
higher and higher
in the sky,
and rabbits burrowing
deeper and deeper –
praise the Lord

cats meditating
for hours on end,
and dogs excitedly
letting us know
another snowfall has
arrived –
praise God

all creation –
praise!

+

We light the candle of music
in this season of waiting,
Composer of all wonders,

for those old standards
which make us smile
at the memory of when
we first heard them

for the hymns we know
by heart and will sing

in the soft candlelight
on Christmas Eve

for the little children who sing carols
taught to them by angels
in the middle of the night.
Amen

Second Saturday of Advent: God who is our balm

The prayers of David son of Jesse are ended.

Psalm 72:20

May we now pray

that those hungering
for justice
will be fed with more
than just crumbs
from our tables
groaning with privilege

that those who
wander the shadows
of fear and loss
will find more than
just candles in windows
to guide them to
new life

that those who
are weakened by
the battering of life
will be gathered up
and cradled in
grace and hope

that our prayers
will have more

than just words
and kind thoughts

but be offered with our
hands
feet
backbones
minds
courage

may we now pray

+

We light the candle of healing
in this season of waiting,
God who is our balm

for those whose hearts
are broken by the ones
they thought were soulmates

for communities divided by
ancient enmities and fears

for little ones whose souls
have been bruised by bullies
Amen

Third Week of Advent

Third Sunday of Advent: Delight of the universes

Good and upright is the Lord;
    therefore he instructs sinners in the way.
He leads the humble in what is right,
    and teaches the humble his way.
All the paths of the Lord are steadfast love and faithfulness,
    for those who keep his covenant and his decrees.

Psalm 25:8–10

Arriving late
for Humility 101,
i slip into the back
row, hoping
you won't notice

putting my notepad
on the desk,
i hold my pen to the
paper so
that it looks like i am
paying rapt attention
and taking copious
notes

making sure to keep my
eyes wide open
and glued to the board
where you are showing
the formula

on how the last
become first,
I daydream of
my nice warm bed

at the end of class,
i turn towards the place where
i can get a refill
on my grande latte,
not noticing my mates
following you to the corner of
Steadfast Love
and
Faithfulness.

+

We light the candle of joy
in this season of waiting,
Delight of the universes,

as we go to make angels
in the snow with kids and dogs

as we walk on beaches
to marvel at your sunsets.
Amen

Third Monday of Advent: Heart of our hearts

I waited patiently for the Lord ...

Psalm 40:1a

Patiently,
i wait
for you to show
me how i can share
from my gifts,
   while impatiently
   switching the channel
   to avoid the stories
   of folk trying to rebuild
   everything after the storms

patiently,
i wait
for you to whisper
the words of hope and grace
for which i hunger,
   while impatiently
   brushing past my neighbour
   trying to share their news

patiently,
i wait for you
to come once again
in this holy season,
   while impatiently

holding a young
stranger's crying baby
while she rummages
in the bag
for a bottle

+

We light the candle of grace
in this season of waiting,
Heart of our hearts,

so that in a world which hears
far too much bitterness and fear,
we might whisper tender words

so that in a time when it seems
we cannot stand each other,
we might wrap others in your hope.
Amen

Third Tuesday of Advent: Imagination beyond compare

Steadfast love and faithfulness will meet;
*   righteousness and peace will kiss each other.*
Faithfulness will spring up from the ground,
*   and righteousness will look down from the sky.*

Psalm 85:10–11

Like the stars
twinkling in the
inky night sky,
righteousness
looks upon us,
brightening the
bleak midwinter

like two friends
meeting
after months apart
in a pandemic,
faithfulness and peace
surround us with arms
which will never
let go again

like a
weary nurse
checking on
his patients in
intensive care,

steadfast love
watches over us
in every
moment.

+

We light the candle of wonder
in this season of waiting,
Imagination beyond compare,

so that when our ears become numbed
by the endless loop of holiday music,
we can still hear the angels rehearsing

so that when our eyes become dimmed
by our favourite movie shown
every six hours on every streaming service,
we can still see the stars –
shooting across the night sky.
Amen

Third Wednesday of Advent: Sharer of your heart's abundance

They heard the sound of the Lord God walking in the garden at the time of the evening breeze, and the man and his wife hid themselves from the presence of the Lord God among the trees of the garden. But the Lord God called to the man, and said to him, 'Where are you?' He said, 'I heard the sound of you in the garden, and I was afraid, because I was naked; and I hid myself.'

Genesis 3:8–10

i want to
walk with you
by my side,
but i am
fearful
that you might want
to go to those places
i try so hard to avoid

i long
to talk with you,
to hear your voice,
but what if
you ask me
to speak words of hope
to those i cannot stand

i believe
you are always
watching over me,

but hope you won't mind
if i occasionally
shut the door,
draw the drapes,
close the blinds and
bring out the bitterness
of my heart to nibble
on as a snack

+

We light the candle of receiving
in this season of waiting,
Sharer of your heart's abundance,

so we may open
our arms to the forgotten
our hands to the lonely
our hearts to the broken
our ears to the voiceless.
Amen

Third Thursday of Advent: Omnipotent God

Paul, a servant of God and an apostle of Jesus Christ, for the sake of the faith of God's elect and the knowledge of the truth that is in accordance with godliness.

Titus 1:1

The broken
no one cares
to fix

the lost
we refuse to
offer directions

the hungry
we deem unworthy
to have even our
leftovers

the forgotten
we turn our eyes
away from

the fallen
we are too busy
to offer a hand

these are
the favoured ones,
the elect,
in God's heart.

+

We light the candle of courage
in this season of waiting,
Omnipotent God,

so that we might become
powerless enough to share
our vulnerability with others

so that we might set aside
our reliance on might
and lean on mercy
more and more.
Amen

Third Friday of Advent: God of those we ignore too often

Let your steadfast love, O Lord, be upon us,
even as we hope in you.

Psalm 33:22

My oldest friend
worry
and i had a sleepover
last night, loving God

today, worry
has filled out the
to-do list for me, even
stapling a second page
to make room for everything
worry thinks should fill my moments

could you send me
a new best friend,
Tender God,

maybe
Hope?

+

We light the candle of loneliness
in this season of waiting,
God of those we ignore too often,

for those babies who continue
to be born into poverty

for all the families fleeing
the forces of fear and hate

for everyone who knows
that the hand which they
have been dealt is a losing one
but that there is One
who will continue to deal
hope and grace from
the bottom of the deck.
Amen

Third Saturday of Advent: God who quilts a people

On that day the remnant of Israel and the survivors of the house of Jacob will no more lean on the one who struck them, but will lean on the Lord, the Holy One of Israel, in truth. A remnant will return, the remnant of Jacob, to the mighty God.

Isaiah 10:20–21

In all the jumbles
of shouted words and
even louder anger,
there is just an echo of
kindness

as evil seems to be
expanding its power base,
gathering all the resentful
while hoping the apathetic
will never notice,
there is good which refuses
to give an inch

in the neighbourhoods where
the forgotten are crammed together,
where the ignored are warehoused
out of sight and out of mind,
a sliver of justice
shines in the shadows

when the times seem
to call for selfishness,

for hoarding as much as we can,
for letting fear become a pandemic,
may we be the ones who
give away grace, love and mercy
until there is just a smidgen left

which is all you need.

+

We light the candle of remnants
in this season of waiting,
for that is all it has ever taken,
a remnant of
hope
grace
peace
justice
love
joy
God who quilts a people,

so may we be
that remnant,
one small piece
of the whole cloth
of that life called
caring.
Amen

Fourth Week of Advent

Fourth Sunday of Advent: God of overflowing intimacy

But just when he had resolved to do this, an angel of the Lord appeared to him in a dream and said, 'Joseph, son of David, do not be afraid to take Mary as your wife, for the child conceived in her is from the Holy Spirit.'

Matthew 1:20

i'm dreaming of ...

communities
where building houses
for families living
on the streets is
more important than
sports arenas

neighbourhoods
filled with
children from every
place on earth,
playing
together in peace

streets
which do not
welcome
drug dealers and
gun wielders

homes
whose residents
live out

justice
peace
and hope

people
who love more
than hate

give more than
take

share more
than hoard.

+

We light the candle of love
in this season of waiting

not that overblown love shown
in movies and books,
but that love which is as fallible
and as foolish as your devotion
to your wandering children

not that love which is about me,
but the love which cares more
for the other, and more for the
community of tenderness
we can become if we but love,
God of overflowing intimacy.
Amen

Fourth Monday of Advent: God who is coming

I wait for the Lord,
*   my soul waits,*
* and in his word I hope;*
my soul waits for the Lord
*   more than those who watch*
*   for the morning,*
*   more than those who watch*
*   for the morning.*

Psalm 130:5–6

In the hurly
and burly of this
season,
i wait …
to see you
in the child sitting
still as can be
for a family picture

in the noise
of all the songs
all the time,
i wait …
for the Spirit
to whisper my name
in the pauses
between the notes

in the tangled
traffic with drivers
snarling at each other,
i wait …
to catch a glimpse
of you
coming
closer to us

in this
season of
impatience

i wait …

+

We light the candle of grumpiness
in this season of waiting,
for time seems to be moving
so slowly
in these endless days,
God who is coming,
with a box of new trainers
with our names on them,
so we'll be able to
sprint to the finish line
ahead of all our worries, cares
and fears.
Amen

Fourth Tuesday of Advent: God of disruption

> *And Mary said,*
> *'My soul magnifies the Lord,*
> *and my spirit rejoices in God my Saviour,*
> *for he has looked with favour on the lowliness of his servant.*
> *Surely, from now on all generations will call me blessed;*
> *for the Mighty One has done great things for me,*
> *and holy is his name.*
> *His mercy is for those who fear him*
> *from generation to generation.*
> *He has shown strength with his arm;*
> *he has scattered the proud in the thoughts of their hearts.*
> *He has brought down the powerful from their thrones,*
> *and lifted up the lowly;*
> *he has filled the hungry with good things,*
> *and sent the rich away empty ...'*

Luke 1:46–55

Our souls play leapfrog
until God and i collapse
onto the soft grass,
laughing in delight

no one else wants
to play with me, but
i am always chosen
to be on God's team

God shows me how
to bend the ball

into the back of the net,
and shares the divine
password with me

God cradles us whenever
the bullies taunt us,
and does the same
for our kids, as well

God tickles the arrogant
until they laugh so hard
they forget their plans

he removes all the chairs
at the same time, and when
the music stops playing,
the proud have
no place to sit
but on the floor,

watching while the forgotten
are seated at the banquet,
piling up their plates with
every tasty treat, while the
rich are handed
empty carrier bags

God gives the compassionate
all the skills and tools they need
to care for those we always ignore,
keeping the vow made at
that wedding so long ago.

+

We light a candle in this season of waiting,
God of disruption,
for families whose identities
do not appear on Christmas cards

for struggling parents who must set aside
their pride so they can get their kids
the help, care and hope they need

for young people whose longing
for creation justice challenges all
who counsel them to just be patient.
Amen

Fourth Wednesday of Advent: God who is speaking to us

Our God comes and does not keep silence ...

Psalm 50:3a

We sing of that silent night,
but you want us to listen
to the whispered prayers
of children hoping for food

to the loneliness of the teen
who sleeps in the back
of a friend's van because
his parents have changed
the locks on their home

to the groaning of creation
suffering from greedy choices
and the wilful ignorance of facts.

+

We light the candle of wisdom
in this season of waiting,
God who is speaking to us,

so that we might discern you
in our midst when we cannot see
or hear you
Amen

Fourth Thursday of Advent: God our love, our voice, our hope

Once God has spoken;
*   twice have I heard this:*
*   that power belongs to God,*
*   and steadfast love belongs to you, O Lord.*

Psalm 62:11–12a

You thundered from
a mountaintop about how
we are to live with others,
and when we did not listen,
you whispered in a mother's
voice as she fed her newborn

you pushed mountains
up out of majestic plains

you flung stars into the night
to inspire artists and poets

then you showed your true strength
by becoming completely dependent
on parents everyone believed
would never amount to anything,
all because of love

your love for us.

+

We light the candle of voices
in this season of waiting
for there are those whose
hopes for justice are never heard
over the platitudes of politicians

for there are children whose
cries of hunger are silenced
by the noise of feasts

for there are those new songs
of love, of peace, of kindness
that are never sung, simply
because they are new,
God our love, our voice, our hope.
Amen

Fourth Friday of Advent: God of compassion

Out of the depths I cry to you, O Lord.
Lord, hear my voice!
*   Let your ears be attentive*
*   to the voice of my supplications!*

Psalm 130:1–2

In our isolation
come to us,
as you did
to the family
hunkered down
in that stable
so long ago

in our fear
come to us,
as you did
to those shepherds
on a hillside
so long ago

in our poverty
of hope
come to us,
as you did
to your people
on that night
so long ago

in the emptiness
of our hearts
come to us,
as you did
in that baby
so long ago

+

We light the candle of patience
in this season of waiting,
God of compassion,
and no matter how many
times we dip our fingertips
into the water of our worries
to snuff it out, may we find
some light
to wrap around
all those on the edge,
who feel like they are about
to fall
and never hit bottom.
Amen

Fourth Saturday of Advent: God of Light

Now the birth of Jesus the Messiah took place in this way. When his mother Mary had been engaged to Joseph, but before they lived together, she was found to be with child from the Holy Spirit. Her husband Joseph, being a righteous man and unwilling to expose her to public disgrace, planned to dismiss her quietly. But just when he had resolved to do this, an angel of the Lord appeared to him in a dream …

Matthew 1:18–20a

i'm dreaming of
a quiet Christmas
in the cacophony
of folk who just cannot
stop shouting and quarrelling

i'm dreaming of
a healing Christmas
for all broken relationships

i'm dreaming of
a gentle Christmas
for all those tossed aside
by a neglectful world

i'm dreaming of
(maybe, just maybe)
another Christmas
just like the first one
so long ago

when you came when
and where we least
expected

+

Light the candle of hope this night
for all who have seen
their dreams come true

light the candle of peace this night
for all whose hands
reach out to enemies

light the candle of joy this night
for little kids (and big)
whose eyes widen
when they realise who was actually born
on that morning so long ago

light the candle of love this night
for everyone welcomed into families
they never knew existed

light the candle of justice this night
to light the candle of courage

light the candle of grace this night
to light the candle of generosity

light all the candles of God's gifts
poured out on us, not just on one night,

or even during one season,
so that they might show us
the path through the shadows
of worry, grief,
oppression and loneliness

Light a candle this night
for the God of Light.
Amen

Christmas Eve

Christmas Eve: Whispering God

Let the same mind be in you that was in Christ Jesus,
who, though he was in the form of God,
*   did not regard equality with God*
*   as something to be exploited,*
but emptied himself ...

Philippians 2:4–7a

In the night's
        silence,
    while we sleep
    dreaming
            of all
        that awaits us
            under the tree,

you
    creep down
    out of heaven,
        so softly
        no motion detector on earth
    could ever sense it,

to burrow
    under the covers,
    swaddling
        us with
        that peace given
            for all,

your grace
  tickling
    cold feet
until we giggle
      with

delight.

+

We're almost there
he whispered in the ear
of the donkey, whose feet hurt
more than his

we're almost there
she whispered to the baby
moving around in her womb

we're almost there
the shepherds whispered
to their flocks at the top of the hill

we're almost there
whispered the angelic host director

we're almost there
you whisper,
whispering God,
as we wait
impatiently.

Christmas Day

Christmas Day: God in community, Holy and One

The one who comes from above is above all; the one who is of the earth belongs to the earth and speaks about earthly things. The one who comes from heaven is above all.

John 3:31

You came
not for the carols
but that we
could hear the weary voices
of healthcare folk
pleading for common
sense

you came
not for homilies
or for liturgies crafted
by wordsmiths
but that we might become
living letters of
the good news
living out lives of
caring and compassion
speaking louder than
any word

you came
so that even in
the midst of another

variant, more lockdowns,
whatever else might come,
we might continue
to incarnate the mystery
of your coming
with deeds of
justice and peace.

+

We light the candles of vision
in this season of waiting,
that we might see you
in the refugees who have travelled
so far to reach a new home

that we might notice you
in the folk sleeping in cars
because there is no room
for them in our prosperity

that we might recognise you
in the person who treats us
with patience and kindness this day,
God in community, Holy and One.
Amen

Meditation

In the days following Christmas, you might like to meditate and ponder on these titles yourself. I hope that the time helps bring you closer to God, the world and others.

God who does cartwheels
God who lights the way
God who never forgets us
God who watches on hillsides
God who is still with us
God of the forgotten
God of grace and sharing
God who never blows out the light
God who tries to slow us down
God whose heart is filled with stained glass in its cracks
God who watches in the night
God of abundant creation
Composer of all wonders
God who is our balm
Delight of the universes
Heart of our hearts
Imagination beyond compare
Sharer of your heart's abundance
Omnipotent God

God of those we ignore too often
God who quilts a people
God of overflowing intimacy
God who is coming
God of disruption
God who is speaking to us
God our love, our voice, our hope
God of compassion
God of Light
Whispering God
God in community, Holy and One

Sources and acknowledgements

About the author

Thom Shuman's first book was 2005's *Jesse Tree* – and since then he has been a much-loved Wild Goose writer. Thom's voice is like no one else's. There's a vulnerability, gentleness and childlike wonder in his writing that folk deeply connect with, and that well fits the Advent and Christmas season.

Thom lives in Columbus, Ohio with his family, and is a 'retired' pastor and an associate member of the Iona Community. His previous books include *How Shall We Pray This Morning? For What Shall We Pray This Night?*, *Grace Will Walk Us Home*, *Christmas Eve in the Diner*, *The Soft Petals of Grace*, and *Gobsmacked*.